I CHING
WISDOM
VOLUME II

MORE GUIDANCE FROM THE
BOOK OF CHANGES

By *wu wei*

Power Press
Los Angeles, California

I CHING WISDOM, Volume II

MORE GUIDANCE FROM THE BOOK OF CHANGES

By *wu wei*

Power Press, 1310 Riviera Ave., Venice, CA 90291
Telephone: (310) 392-9393
Fax (310) 392-7710
Website: www.power-press.com
Email to *wu wei*: wuwei@power-press.com

Library of Congress Card Number 94-66782
ISBN 0-943015-29-4
Copyright © 1998 Power Press
First Edition
10 9 8 7 6 5 4 3 2

Author's Apology to Women Readers

I sincerely apologize for using *he, his, him* when speaking generally. Using *he/she* throughout becomes cumbersome for the reader and disturbs the flow of thought. I chose to use the masculine form because it is what we are accustomed to seeing in print and because the goal is to make the reading easy.

Author's Apology to All Readers

There are several sayings in this book that are similar to sayings that are to be found in I Ching Wisdom, Volume I. They are included here because global economic indications and the cyclical nature of the Universe lead me to believe that the people of the world are soon going to experience financially difficult times. Some of the similar sayings give guidance in preparing for that difficult time, others for inspiration to sustain ourselves within that time, and others for making the most of the time of recovery. Even though a few of the sayings are similar, the comments appended to the sayings are different and further expand the meaning of the thought behind the saying. I humbly apologize to you and ask you to call upon your generosity and greatness of spirit to forgive the redundancy.

Your insignificant servant,
-wu wei

Author's Comment

The sayings in this book are volatile. I use the word *volatile* because one of the meanings of volatile is, "having the power to fly." These volatile sayings from the I Ching have the potential of giving us the power to fly, to break us loose from that which holds us in place, to help us to reach lofty goals, to provide the means for us to soar to the heights of success and good fortune, and to show us how to recognize and avoid the pitfalls that beset the path of the unenlightened. We should take them to heart, treat them as we would a great treasure, cherish them as we would a dear child, and then, when we have made them our own, natural law will prevail, the miracle will occur, the promise will be fulfilled, and we will be able to steer a safer, clearer course through the uncharted journey of our lives, mounting to the skies of success as though on the wings of six dragons.

Your servant,

-wu wei

Author's Request

Throughout this book reference is made to the superior person. I humbly request that you do not permit yourself to be put off by the term. Today, thousands of years beyond the time when the term was frequently on the lips of the sages, we have a tendency to think of "the superior person" as one who puts on airs, who is overly impressed with himself. In ancient times the term was used to denote a person of lofty character, of great wisdom, of good intentions, of noble thoughts, and, above all, of humility, humble as only a great sage can be humble. He was looked up to, respected, yes, even honored and revered. I have used the term in the manner of the ancients, and I ask your great indulgence by taking the term to heart, and not thinking poorly of me for it, nor taking me to task for my inability to think of a better term. Please begin by reading the characteristics of the superior person at the back of this book.

Your insignificant and humble servant,

-wu wei

Fu Hsi rising from the mountain designing the eight great signs.

1

*To be joyous of heart
is the way of the superior person.* [*]

wu wei's comment:

Holding joy in our hearts attracts friends, creates harmony within ourselves and others, creates an inner sense of well-being, and puts a sparkle in our eyes. To be joyous of heart is to hold an optimistic outlook, to see adversity as opportunity, to see failure as the starting point of success, to view our stubbed toes as the release of acupuncture points, to wake with a feeling of gratitude, and to sleep with a sustaining, unfaltering trust in the Universe of which we are a part. The person with a joyous heart is a treasure to be with, a wellspring of inspiration, and a fit companion. When we are joyous of heart, we hear a resonance in the songs of the birds, see resonance in the opening of a flower, and feel it in the pressure of a friend's hand.

---

[*] See the last few pages of this book regarding the superior person.

*Male and female
are not opposite sexes.*

wu wei's comment:

They are not opposite but complimentary. The meaning of opposite is generally thought to be opposing, and from that arises misconceptions about the true relationship of men and women. In the Universe, the Creative force, symbolized by the male energy, brings things into being, but to do so, it must work through the Receptive force, symbolized by the female energy. Neither the Receptive force nor the Creative force can do anything without the other. It follows that a woman is the perfect compliment to a man as a man is the perfect compliment to a woman, not opposing each other, but complimenting each other, each assisting the other to rise to greater heights than he or she could have alone. Those who understand that concept and live by it will enjoy the benefits and happiness one can experience in the company of their complimentary mates.

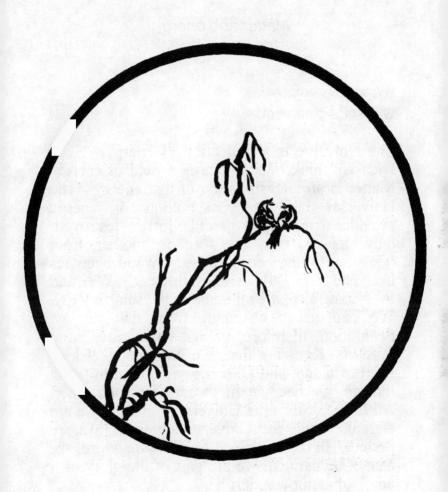

3

Matter and energy
are one.

wu wei's comment:

The Universe is a collection of energy. Even what we think of as space is a field of energy. Matter is an intensification of that energy. The Universal law of conservation of energy provides that energy cannot be lost or destroyed; only changed from one form to another, from one state to another, as flaming wood becomes heat and sunlight becomes flowers. We, and everything else, are all made of the same energy. We can never be apart from that energy. Separation, therefore, in that basic way, is an illusion. Knowing that, we need not feel lost, apart or alone, and knowing separation to be an illusion, we become fit to care for each other. All *is* one. Since the Universe is eternal, we are eternal. Since the Universe is perfect, we are perfect. In the Universal sense of the word, we cannot be harmed; we are part of the glory of it all. Is that not wonderful?

*We create the world
by our expectations.*

wu wei's comment:

Thinking the world a selfish place, we find selfishness. Selfishness is what we expect, what we look for, and, consequently, what we find. Having found it, and seeing our beliefs confirmed, we say to ourselves, "I knew it." Thinking the world a generous place, we find generosity. Believing ourselves capable, we set out toward accomplishment; believing ourselves incapable, we fail to begin. If we knew we were creating the world by our expectations, would we not create expectations that would lead us to the realization of our fondest dreams? This is the time for us to recall our unrealized dreams and hold them clearly in our minds. Just by holding them thus, we have already started them on their way into the physical realm. We are far more powerful than we believe, and everything of which we conceive is within our grasp.

Do not despair.

wu wei's comment:

Times of despair come to us all—times when troubles seem about to overwhelm us and hopelessness fills us with despair. Our belief that there is no hope or help is only a false illusion. Of course, hope and help are available, and in sufficient quantity to cure even the greatest problem. And more than just hope, there is certainty, if the truth be known, that the time of trouble will pass to be replaced by a time of joy. The difficult part is keeping aware in the time of trouble that it is only temporary. It is an eternal law of life that we must all pass through the fire, for that is where strength is gained, endurance enhanced, and the secrets of our hearts revealed to us, but it is also true that all times of trouble are followed by times of gladness. Therefore, be of good cheer and do not despair. We are all in the hands of a loving Universe of which we are a part.

11

People of true understanding
nourish sages
and through them,
nourish the whole world.

wu wei's comment:

A truly wise person, perceiving a sage, extends
him hospitality and nourishment, provides for
his needs, and sees to his comfort. The sage,
having had his needs cared for, is then able to
instruct 10,000 others who, in their turn, nourish
the whole world. It is only a few who will
understand the value of these words and act
upon them, but for those few, heaven's blessings
will descend upon them as does a warm spring
rain upon flowers, and, as the rain nourishes the
flowers and causes them to prosper and flourish,
so those good souls will spend their days in
contentment and happiness, and their nights in
restful, peaceful sleep, for they have nourished
the world through a sage. That is the way.

*Faith is stronger
than so-called reality.*

wu wei's comment:

It is *so-called* reality because while it appears
real, it is only our perception of it. When five
people stand around a pond and point to the
moon's reflection, everyone points to a different
spot on the surface of the water. One person
sees an event as a benefit, another sees the same
event as a loss. Those of us who have walked
through the fire of life and found that
misfortune, loss, and adversity are an ultimate
fiction, have discovered that each event, no
matter how dire, holds a gift for us. We have
experienced the ultimate nature of the Universe
and found it to be loving. Even in the grip of
calamitous misfortune, grievous loss, or supreme
adversity, we know it is all for our benefit.
Acting in accord with what we know, reality
shapes itself accordingly. When we attain that
level, even the flowers, the stones, and the
animals know us as we pass by.

*Everything comes
at the appointed time.*

wu wei's comment:

It is not necessary to have all the ingredients of a project in hand at the outset—they will come at the appointed time. It is only important that we move forward with the project until that appointed time arrives. Neither is it necessary to fret over the late arrival of another, for we can only arrive at the appointed time. All that is necessary is that we attend to our own state of mind until the appointed time of arrival has come.

9

*The forces of light and dark
fluctuate constantly.*

wu wei's comment:

The forces of good and evil, negative and positive, wax and wane incessantly and proportionately, the decrease of one resulting in an increase of the other, as in day to night or full to empty. During the time of the ascendancy of the light force, good fortune smiles upon us. When the dark force prevails, misfortune draws near. One of the greatest benefits of using the I Ching as a tool of divination is to discover the time of the light force and the dark, and to act accordingly. To thrust ahead during the time of the dark force is the way of the imprudent, and he who takes action at that time invites misfortune. To make progress during the time of the light force is the way of the wise, and he who takes action at that time realizes his goals and soars to the heights of success as swiftly as cheetahs over the plain.

19

In the hands of an inferior person
even the finest plan
comes to naught.

wu wei's comment:

Every plan in which we participate has one constant, ourselves. Not that we are always the same, but that we are always part of the plan. All else comes and goes: friends, parents, possessions, conditions, situations, and associates, leaving only us, ourselves. If we are inferior people and cannot depend on ourselves for assets such as endurance, effectiveness, trustworthiness, or loyalty, even our best plans will have the potential of being fatally flawed, and it would be better for us if we undertook nothing. When we walk the path of the superior person, we may undertake any project, reach any goal, and attain greatness, Universal law bringing about the only possible end, sublime success. Is it not wise therefore to cultivate strong character?

11

For every action
there is a reaction
which is in perfect accord
with the action.

wu wei's comment:

That is the most basic law of the Universe—cause and effect. If our actions are the result of our intentions to do good, to create harmony, to deal fairly, to love dearly, and to live the life of the superior person, can anything else happen except that, as a result of natural law, we reach the loftiest goals to which one can attain and lead lives of greatest happiness?

*Once we have developed ourselves
and formed our characters,
we will be tempered in the fire of life.*

wu wei's comment:

The fire of life is the Universal force that endlessly shapes and alters us until we come to realize who we are in relationship to the rest of the Universe, and learn to act accordingly. Usually, the altering process takes the form of adversity, and, as far as outward appearances are concerned, seems to be working against us, when, actually, it is working for us. To see each of those instances for what they are, opportunities for growth and improvement, is the way of the sage. Seeing them in that light will bring an amazing change in our outlooks, for we will then see all obstacles and adversities as opportunities, and we consequently lose our resentment of them. For being successful in that endeavor, we will be profoundly rewarded by the Universe.

Once the Universe was created,
everything became possible.

wu wei's comment:

The greatest deed was the accomplishment of the Universe. Once that was accomplished, everything else became possible, even easy, relatively speaking. By bringing about the manifestation of our conceptions, we build character, learn of life, experience existence and grow in every way. Knowing that all things are possible expands our horizons, increases our options, and extends our goals to include even the seemingly impossible. When we come to the full realization of that, we can act on our own initiatives, move confidently forward, let loose our power, and soar upward. Casting anxious hesitation aside, we can rise to the greatest heights imaginable. We need not fear for we *are* the Universe.

The person of good conduct
finds an easy path through the world.

wu wei's comment:

A person shows good conduct by acting in a manner appropriate to each situation. He is courteous, mannerly, and non-offensive in situations that call for such conduct, and he is aggressive, deliberate and courageous when that type of conduct is indicated. A person of good conduct earns our admiration, and we should, as far as possible without losing our own identities, imitate him. When we use good conduct, no resentment arises against us, and our forward progress is smooth and easy. People admire, respect, and look up to us when we have mastered the art of good conduct. For our demonstration of good conduct, we will be sought after, and many fine opportunities will come our way.

15

Fear and courage
go hand in hand.

wu wei's comment:

When there is nothing to fear, courage is
unnecessary. * Courage is what we call upon to
face what we fear. If we permit fear to run
through us without awakening our courage, our
fear grows, and we are blocked from taking
action, paralyzed. Fear is not within the
situation or object we fear, but exists solely
within us, within our imaginations—it is our
expectations of a bad outcome. What we fear
dies or fades away after we have faced what we
feared. Wonderfully, the Universe has provided
each of us with enough courage to face even our
darkest fear. It is a sad moment indeed when
we succumb to our fear without having called
upon our courage, for when we call upon it, we
become as brave as the Chinese temple dogs of
ancient China who were selected for their
extraordinary bravery to protect the temples.

---

* See wu wei's I Ching Handbook, Chapter 7.

Moment by moment,
we mold our futures.

wu wei's comment:

Our thoughts produce our actions, which, in accord with Universal law, produce effects. The effects become, for us, the future. By acting as superior people, we create effects that make wonderful futures for ourselves, futures that bring us great happiness. Holding evil thoughts produces evil actions which creates stress and produces an acid in our systems, lines in our faces and hate in our hearts. Holding loving thoughts, nourishing thoughts, produces actions that bring us tranquillity and peace and provides us with soft, radiant countenances.

17

When two people are at one
in their inmost hearts,
they shatter even the strength of iron
or of bronze.

wu wei's comment:

2500 years ago, Confucius, seven feet tall, with a lumpy head and coarse features, spoke those beautiful words as part of a poem*. When two people, be they partners, lovers, husband and wife, or participants in any other relationship, attain sufficient depth in their relationship so that complete trust and understanding reign, they may undertake any goal, confront any danger, survive any hardship, and reach the heights of sublime success without a misstep. They are each fit to care for the other, and each is a continual source of joy and nourishment for the other. Such a relationship is worth 10,000 kingdoms.

---

* See page 164 for entire poem.

To arouse enthusiasm in a group,
it is necessary to adjust our attitudes
to the character of the group.

wu wei's comment:

If we speak intellectually to people of lesser understanding, we lose our audience. If we speak loftily to people of base mentality, we fail in our efforts. To lead people or influence them, we must first align ourselves with them. By identifying with individuals or groups, we gain their confidence and can then lead them into a higher understanding or direct them to the achievement of lofty goals. Anyone who understands that concept and employs it can easily enlist the aid of helpers, influence small or large groups of people, and thereby attain success.

19

Natural law is easy to follow
because it operates
along the path of least resistance.

wu wei's comment:

In the I Ching, the two primary forces of the Universe are called The Creative, which brings things into being, and The Receptive, through which The Creative works. The Creative works through what is easy, the Receptive works through what is simple. The Creative works effortlessly because it guides infinitesimal movements at their first appearance. The Receptive works through what is simple by being purely receptive, never offering the slightest resistance to the Creative. When we keep things easy, others understand them easily, when we keep things simple, others follow them easily. By we, ourselves, remaining easy to know and simple to follow, we will gain many friends and followers and we will attain great success.

20

Doubt not.

wu wei's comment:

All of life is one action following another, interspersed by periods of rest. If we are in doubt about the outcome of our actions, if our thoughts are concerned with, "What if I should fail?" we will be filled with hesitancy, uncertainty, and our actions will lack the conviction needed to obtain a decisive, favorable outcome. Even the worst outcome we can imagine will ultimately benefit us. It is because of that law of favorability that the Universe is able to continue and we are able to bring about the fruition of our plans. Acting with certainty, if we are to act at all, with joy in our hearts, knowing we are Universally supported, will put our wildest dreams and our fondest hopes, yes, even the seemingly impossible, within our grasp. All it takes is that we put our trust in our aware Universe. Is that not a great treasure?

If we would have our rules followed,
we must not violate
the human rights of the people.

wu wei's comment:

When rules are made that are too strict or that
go against what we believe to be in our highest
and best interest or that violate our basic human
rights, we break the rules, and in doing so,
become criminals. When governments tax too
much, they create nations of cheaters. When we
are kept on too short a reign, we break free.
When the rules become too oppressive,
revolution occurs. A well run state is barely
perceptible; the people, being guided by a gentle
hand, are hardly aware they are being governed,
and, as a result, everyone is content, and those
in government are praised.

Music eases tension from the heart,
releases thoughts from the mind,
and inspires us to greatness.

wu wei's comment:

Great music stops the inner turmoil of thought and allows the mind to seek its natural state of joy. Music frees our minds and allows us to soar to heights where we can experience the celestial. Music opens our minds to allow the perception of new thoughts of a higher nature, which gives us a spiritual lift, which produces yet more joy. Every day should find us spending some time giving ourselves over to some great composer whose music lifts us into the rarefied atmosphere of the angels, where the turmoil of our minds grows quiet, our thoughts soar, and we merge with All-That-Is.

23

It is who we think we are
who speaks and acts—not who we are.

wu wei's comment:

When one walks into a room, who that person thinks he is walks into the room, and who he thinks he is speaks. If he thinks himself to be less than fair, loyal, trustworthy, considerate, or moral, he has a diminished self-image, and his attitude and demeanor reflect that. A diminished self-image causes us to slouch, to avoid looking others in the eye, to be unassertive, to be indecisive. On the other hand, a healthy self-image causes us to carry ourselves well, to speak confidently and to portray dignity. If we have not taken the time and thought to create a wonderful self-image for ourselves, we have had less, been less, and done less than was possible for us than if we had. We can improve our self-images at any moment including this one*.

---

* See wu wei's I Ching Handbook, Chapter 2

If we would have our work endure,
we must endow it
with organic Universal principles.

wu wei's comment:

Organic Universal principles regarding work are these: that we do the absolute best we can, that we complete the work in every detail, that the work is performed with love, even if it is just the love of the work, that it is endowed with the joy of creativity, and that when it is finished, we are completely satisfied with it. Working in that manner causes the work to endure. Working in that fashion also causes what we work on to work on us. When we polish an exterior surface to the maximum limits of our potential, our own interior surfaces are polished as well. As we repair a tool, a relationship, a garment, doing it as well as we can, we are repaired. As we endow our work with durability, so we endure.

25

In social intercourse,
one should not try to be all-knowing.

wu wei's comment:

A person who speaks as if he knows everything soon drives away his listeners. The Universe communicates itself to us in many ways, and sometimes, it is through the words of others. If we act the know-it-all, others may refrain from talking to us, and we may fail to get the message they could have given us. We should be open to what others have to say, even encouraging. It is more important that we listen to others than to be always speaking, for in that way we learn what there is to know. We should be easy to talk to, and grateful for new information. Acting in that manner, we will not only gain the information we need, we will also convince people of our modesty, and as a result, we shall arrive at our goals as swiftly as arrows shot from a strong bow.

26

*If we would seek to influence others,
we should follow the true inclination of our
hearts.*

wu wei's comment:

Any deliberate action we take to influence
others that does not arise from a sincere desire
to benefit them loses innocence and therefore
becomes a manipulation. If we seek to gain
another's loyalty by manipulation, we must
continue the manipulation after his loyalty is
won or else we will lose it. Such actions are
tiresome, stresses our hearts, and bring an
inevitably poor outcome. To attract people
naturally, effortlessly, we need only follow the
true prompting of our hearts. Of such stuff are
true leaders made.

27

Everything clings
to that which gives it life.

wu wei's comment:

As plants cling to the earth for nourishment, as fire clings to wood for fuel, as infants cling to their mothers' breasts for food, so we, being spiritual creatures, must cling to our spiritual source if we are to prosper. Our spiritual source is the Universe. It lends magical power to our lives. By revering it, communicating with it, and acknowledging it, we are cherished by it, and so attain the greatest states that mortals can desire. Close your eyes, draw a deep breath, and know that you have just inhaled the life force, the power, the awareness, and the consciousness of the Universe. Just being who we are at any moment is the greatest spiritual experience we can have. Those words contain a portion of the ancient wisdom handed down to us from 10,000 years ago. Pondering those words for their inner meaning brings great wisdom.

28

In teaching,
everything depends on consistency.

wu wei's comment:

If the teacher's words and conduct are not in
accord with his teaching, the student may fail to
credit the lesson with validity, and the teaching
may not have any beneficial effect upon him. It
is also true that the failure of the student is the
failure of the teacher, and whichever one
discounts that lesson is as far off the track as the
other.

29

In the Universe,
we are always exactly on time.

wu wei's comment:

The Universe was created at exactly the right
moment to allow for the creation of our planet
and solar system. The earth cooled at exactly
the right moment to allow for the evolution of
life forms. We were born, each of us, at exactly
the right moment to allow us to arrive at this
moment in time. Everything that happens,
happens at the only possible time it can happen,
and it is always at exactly the right time. We
cannot get to an appointment before we
arrive—or after. It is only at the instant of our
arrival that we can arrive, and that is always at
exactly the right moment, the perfect moment,
the only possible moment. Universal law will
not permit it to be otherwise. So, we can
relax—in the Universe, we are always on time.

30

In the Universe,
we are always in exactly the right place.

wu wei's comment:

When the Universe was formed, everything was
used up.   There is no box hidden away
somewhere in which can be found leftover
mountains, galaxies, suns, people, or waterfalls.
Everything was used, and it was in exactly the
right place—and still is—including us. We are
always at the perfect place, at the perfect time,
to experience the perfect event, for our perfect
understanding, which is for our perfect growth.
Knowing that can help keep us perfectly sane
and perfectly happy under even the most trying
of times.

31

Rest must follow activity
if energy is to be renewed.

wu wei's comment:

The principle of allowing energy that is renewing itself to be provided with rest applies to all situations such as health after illness, understanding after estrangement, winter rest after summer growth, peace after war, prosperity after famine, and rest after exertion. Without the required period of rest, sufficient energy for sustained renewal will be lacking, and failure may occur. At the beginning of the period of rest, everything must be treated tenderly and with great care, so the return may lead to a flowering. He who heeds these words will live long and well, fulfilling his goals with ease.

32

Evil
eventually destroys
itself.

wu wei's comment:

The nature of evil is destructive. Therefore, anyone who employs it to gain his ends is always himself damaged by it. That is part of Universal law. It is also true that when evil, being a purely destructive force, finds nothing left to conquer, it turns upon itself and succeeds in its final conquest.

33

*The greatest honor one can have
is to be part of the Universe.*

wu wei's comment:

We are part of a living, conscious, aware, creative Universe, so awesomely huge that even with our most powerful radio telescopes we can only see an infinitesimal part of it and can only speculate about its immensity. We, as part of it, are able to live, to think, to do, to create, to bring about change, to bring forth other humans, and to expend and renew energy. Everything has consciousness, but in the entire Universe we are the only life form of which we know that has been gifted with this degree of consciousness, this degree of awareness. It is an honor beyond anything imaginable and far exceeds any honor that any human can bestow upon us. Therefore, there is no need for us to think poorly of ourselves or to ever feel rejected, for we have been selected to receive the greatest honor of all.

34

Words
cannot completely express thoughts.

wu wei's comment:

We can describe a horse, but we cannot say what a horse actually is. Feelings particularly are difficult to convey in words. We can say we love someone, but that word means something different to us all. We have the best chance of communicating our thoughts if we are sincere and speak from the heart, without hidden intent. In communication, intent is the key word. If we intend to speak truthfully, sincerely, without flattery or trickery, without any intent to deceive, we have the best chance of communicating our thoughts. It benefits us to learn to love the ring of words that tell the truth, for in that love lies our best chance of being understood and believed. He who follows these precepts will live deep in the wellspring of life, tasting its greatest pleasures, savoring its greatest gifts. He, indeed, will be at the core of life.

35

*Misfortune, good fortune,
embarrassment, praise, and regret
are purely the result of our conduct.*

wu wei's comment:

The happy person, the cheerless person, the person of abundance and the pauper, all have arrived at their respective states of mind as the direct result of their prior conduct—of being who they were. Some of the most learned among us attribute failure and success, gain and loss to luck or chaos—out-of-control, random chance. Those who believe in chaos do not see a big enough picture to be able to put chaos into its proper perspective of perfect order. Believing in chaos takes away our power, imbues our best efforts with a chance of failure, and destroys faith in a cause and effect Universe. Chaos is only a way of describing that which we do not understand. Do not be misled—living the life of the superior person results in a superior life—always.

36

The wisest among us
bases his philosophy
on that which is true in the Universe.

wu wei's comment:

A philosophy is a theory of the principles and laws that regulate the Universe and that underlie all knowledge and all reality. It is what we believe to be true about our Universe and everything in it. If our philosophies are based on a belief that is inconsistent with reality, our judgments and decisions will be flawed. Strong philosophies, based on what is true in the Universe, will guide us through the difficult times of adversity and despair that seem to occur regularly in all our lives and will brighten and make better even the best of good times. Those of us whose philosophies are based on the belief that the Universe is alive, aware, and well inclined, and that we are part of it, will find our philosophies of sufficient strength and validity to see us through all the rigors and tests of time. From that belief alone will come the rest of the truth.

37

In seeking advice from others
it is always wise to listen carefully
to what they have to say.

wu wei's comment:

In seeking advice, we are either looking for confirmation of what we believe to be our best course of action or for an alternative idea. When the advice we receive is contradictory to our own thoughts, we sometimes do not listen carefully enough to perceive the value of what is being said. It is the alternatives which have the potential to give us the greatest help, either by providing us with a new plan or by confirming in our minds the wisdom of our own plan. We should, therefore, listen carefully to advice, and study it thoroughly, looking for ways to make use of it. By proceeding in that manner, we have the greatest possibility of achieving success, and by listening carefully, we honor those from whom seek advice and, as an extra benefit, win their respect.

38

*At the commencement of any great
undertaking,*
*the prudent person first determines whether he
is equal to the task and if there are sufficient
assets on hand to attain the goal.*

wu wei's comment:

It is unwise to drain ourselves or our reserves to the point of danger. When we overreach ourselves we risk losing even that which we already have, and in being cautious we avoid the regret that comes from being imprudent. It is also true that we are powerful beyond anything we believe, and even with limited assets and meager power, can reach great goals. Before attempting what is beyond our reach, we should assess the possible gain and the possible loss to see if the risk is worthwhile, and if we find it to be so, we should proceed confidently and courageously, putting anxious hesitation behind us. Finding the risk to be too great, we should prudently seek another alternative.

39

The inferior person,
seeing no advantage,
makes no effort.

wu wei's comment:

A person who sees a way to help another but does not do so because he sees no advantage in it for himself, is, according to the ancient sages, an inferior person. His limited point of view defeats him. He does not know that he would be greatly rewarded by the Universe for helping another, particularly if there was no obvious benefit to himself for doing so. The person who desires to leave things better than he found them, who does more than his share, who is not attached to rewards, who is always seeking to benefit others, who knows he is cared for and rewarded by the Universe for his every effort, is able to act selflessly, without expectation of a reward or a return, without thought of advantage, and of him it is said, "He is better than the best," and, of course, he is greatly rewarded.

40

Be living,
not dying.

wu wei's comment:

Generosity leads to living, stinginess to dying.
Love leads to living, hate to dying. Enthusiasm
leads to living, complaining to dying. Playing
the hero leads to living, playing the victim to
dying. Hope leads to living, hopelessness to
dying. Cheerfulness leads to living, down-
heartedness to dying. Faith leads to living,
faithlessness to dying.

So what e'er you do
And where e'er you go,
No matter how hard or trying,
Keep living in mind
And you will find,
You'll always
Be living,
Not dying.

41

*Things are not
what they seem.*

wu wei's comment:

It is easy to see what is obvious, not so easy to
see what is hidden. An event occurs that brings
great good fortune. The event is obvious; what
is not so obvious is the Universal force which
caused the event to occur. An event occurs and
seemingly brings misfortune. The event is
obvious; what is not so obvious is the Universal
force that caused the event to occur, and what is
even less obvious is that the same force will
cause the event to be for our complete and total
benefit. The master sees beyond what is
obvious. He sees the unseen, feels the unfelt,
and hears the unheard. He looks below the
surface for what is hidden and so finds the great
heartbeat of the Universe. He smiles, knowing
it is his heartbeat, your heartbeat, our heartbeat.

42

That which we want
wants us.

wu wei's comment:

That is the Universal law of attraction. Everything has consciousness, and like attracts like. To have anything we want, we need only raise our level of consciousness to the level of consciousness where what we want exists. It is like being in the elevator of a great department store where all we want exists on successively higher floors. When we have risen to the proper level, what we want is there, waiting for us. To raise our level of consciousness, we focus our attention on becoming aware of the Universe, its consciousness and awareness, and our oneness with it. We then communicate with it, walk within its awareness, acknowledging it at all times. Natural law does the rest. After we have obtained what we want, it is wise to keep in mind that if we allow our level of consciousness to sink, the same law that brought us what we wanted will remove it from us.

43

Do not be deluded that the object
or the success we desire
is the end-all be-all of life.

wu wei's comment:

What we desire, what we work for, or what we
seek after, are those things that merely lead us
along the paths of our lives. It is the paths
themselves that are the end-all and the be-all of
life, for it is on those paths where we shall learn
the lessons we have chosen for this lifetime,
where we shall perfect ourselves as divine
incarnations, where we shall find enlightenment,
where our hopes will be realized and our fears
overcome, and where life will unfold in all its
wonder. Let that path find us wandering along it
filled with anticipation for the next turning, the
next moment, cherishing every event as it
unfolds, and filled with reverence for All-That-
Is.

44

Universal law provides
that everything changes
except Universal law.

wu wei's comment:

Change is like a river: nothing is the same, even for an instant. Everything is continually moving through the six stages of change: about to come into being, beginning, expanding, approaching maximum potential, peaking, and finally, passing its peak and flowing into its new condition. For us to be successful, and in harmony with the world around us, it is imperative that we stay in step with the changes by always acknowledging the rightness, the perfection of the changes, while adapting ourselves to the changes and keeping aware that they are for our complete benefit. He who understands that concept will live as only the fabled kings of old lived, and he will be sublimely successful, sublimely peaceful, and sublimely happy.

45

When closely related people
do not harmonize,
misfortune results.

wu wei's comment:

When people quarrel, they are actually seeking
harmony, although it may not appear so. Each is
trying to mold the other into a form with which
each is compatible. Quarreling is a poor way to
achieve harmony, but if the participants have not
learned a better way, that is all that is left to
them. In business, disharmony results in
ineffectiveness, in a stressful workplace. In a
family, disharmony results in a stressful home,
in a poor living environment within which it is
difficult for its members to flourish. In any type
of organization, disharmony is crippling. To
undertake great projects there must be unity, for
it is only with unity that a concentrated effort
can be made. Strive to be harmonious, overlook
the faults of others, their failings and
shortcomings, and forgive even deliberate
misdeeds. Universal law will then bring great
good fortune and success.

46

To achieve great happiness and success,
it is essential to know what is enough.

wu wei's comment:

What is the point in our continuing after the goal
has been reached? Why should we continue to
eat after we are full? Why should we continue
to amass wealth after we have enough to sustain
ourselves? The Universal law of increase and
decrease provides that everything, when it
reaches its maximum potential, turns toward its
opposite. Therefore, those wisest among us
stop before having too much, doing too much, or
wanting too much, before the limit is reached.
In that way we do not over-extend ourselves,
strive foolishly, or waste effort that could be
better spent in another area of our lives. By
limiting ourselves in that manner, we will find
that we always have time for everything, that
peace reigns in our lives, and that we will
experience contentment.

47

*Life and death
are part of one
recurring cycle.*

wu wei's comment:

To become light, something must first be dark;
to become dark, something must first be light.
To become big, something must first be small; to
become small, something must first be big.
To become hot, something must first be cold; to
become cold, something must first be hot.
To become dead, something must first be alive;
to become alive, something must first be dead.

That is the way. Light and dark are both
degrees of illumination. Bigger and smaller are
both degrees of measurement. Hot and cold are
both degrees of temperature. Life and death are
both degrees of existence. Be happy and of
good faith, for we are indestructible children of
an eternal Universe.

48

To preserve what we have,
we should give
generously.

wu wei's comment:

To preserve our relationships, we give of our time, our assets, our attention, our help, and our love. To preserve our wealth, we give generously as we are accumulating, so we do not invoke the Universal law of maximization, which states that when anything reaches its maximum potential, it turns toward its opposite. Each of us, to be loved, cherished, and valued, should dispense wisdom, love, assets, consideration, and help—generously. By doing so, we will be added to in every beneficial way. Neither will we attract resentment, and no one will hinder us, but all will seek to benefit us.

49

In forming groups,
membership must be open to all
if they are to be successful.

wu wei's comment:

To form one group based on the condemnation
of another group is narrow-minded indeed. It
demonstrates a lack of understanding of
Universal law, which does not exclude anyone.
Certainly, whom the Universe has deemed
worthy of inclusion should be worthy of our
meager inclusion as well. For acting in that
manner, which is in accord with the highest
Universal principles, the groups we form shall
have the best chance of prospering.

50

*Enlightenment is the key
to the Universal treasure chest.*

wu wei's comment:

Yogis spend years meditating in their efforts to experience enlightenment. Students of Zen concentrate for years on koans, Zen problems, in their efforts to experience enlightenment. Having attained their goal, the enlightened ones attest that the experience came in a flash and lasted but an instant, but was so powerful that it changed them forever. What they experienced that was so powerful is their oneness with the Universe. That is what enlightenment is: knowing that everything in the Universe is created from and is part of the same energy, and knowing in what way we relate to it all. Once that awareness is obtained, all else falls into place, everything makes sense, and everything can be understood. That is why enlightenment is the key to the Universal treasure chest.

51

The path to enlightenment
is different
for each of us.

wu wei's comment:

Every spider web is different from every other spider web. The face of every person is different from every other face. No leaf is the same as any other leaf. Everything is different from everything else—the diversification is total. Can we not therefore surmise that the path to enlightenment is different for every person? Must be different? The path that one person follows is not the correct path for any other person. Each of us must walk his own path to enlightenment—that is the way.

52

We cannot be off our paths
to enlightenment.

wu wei's comment:

Enlightenment is like an ocean. Our paths to enlightenment are like rivers. Each river is different, but all rivers eventually lead to the ocean. No matter what it is we are doing, or when, whether it brings us happiness or remorse, gain or loss, we are all on our individual paths to enlightenment. Even when we believe we have done something wrong, we are still on our individual paths to enlightenment. The progress we make along our paths will be quick or slow according to our intentions. By our intentionally seeking enlightenment, which manifests as a desire to discover our relationship with the Universe and our individual roles within it, we will progress quickly, enjoying the commensurate rewards of peace, success, possessions, great good fortune, and well-being. But even the worst and most unenlightened among us is on his path to enlightenment. That is the way.

53

*If we do not heed Universal lessons
life becomes ever more difficult.*

wu wei's comment:

As a loving parent must sometimes discipline a
wayward child with ever stricter measures until
the child learns not to run into the street, or
touch the flame, so we, if we do not pay
attention to the more subtle prompting of the
Universe, will receive ever stricter lessons until
we learn to live the lives of superior people.

54

Catastrophe
is a Universal tap on the shoulder.

wu wei's comment:

Earthquakes, tornadoes, hurricanes, tidal waves, financial upsets, great loss, severe personal trauma, and emotional shock are all brought about by the Universe. Those cataclysmic events are taps on the shoulder, reminders to us that the Universe is an awesome place and sometimes can be terrifying. The wisest person feels reverence at those times and examines his life to see if his affairs are in order and if he is living the life of the superior person. That is the great value of those events.

55

Commitment,
to be fulfilled,
must be constantly renewed.

wu wei's comment:

We make a commitment to reach a goal—excellent. But to fulfill the commitment it is necessary that we renew it in our minds each time we think of our goal, that we renew our determination to attain victory. Rest is essential, but during our periods of rest, we must think to ourselves that in resting we are renewing our energy to fulfill our commitment. That is what true commitment is: it constantly renews itself until the goal is fulfilled, the destination reached. When we are capable of that kind of commitment, we can reach any goal, arrive at any destination, and undertake even dangerous and difficult projects without fear of failure.

56

Peaceful and calm,
the superior person
achieves a quiet heart.

wu wei's comment:

One of the greatest attributes we can achieve is
a quiet heart. Having a quiet heart means that
we are at peace, that striving has been laid
aside, that we feel safe, and that we are
confident of the future. Having achieved a quiet
heart, we can then turn our attention to the
outside world, where we will be able to see
through the tumult and struggle of life to the
peace that lies within. A quiet-hearted person
awakes with a smile on his lips and an eagerness
in his heart for the day ahead.

57

A relationship formed
because of a common interest,
lasts only so long as the common interest
lasts.

wu wei's comment:

If we put our trust or expectations in the
continuation of a relationship that was formed
for a common purpose, we may be disappointed
because after the purpose has been achieved,
unless some new purpose arises to cause the
continuation of the relationship, it will most
likely end.

58

The superior person
reduces that which is too much
and adds to that which is too little.

wu wei's comment:

It is the excesses and insufficiencies of life that destroy us. It is in balance alone that life can be lived to the fullest, where joy is obtained and where happiness resides.

59

To discipline a youth
brings good fortune.

wu wei's comment:

Even the very young must be taught to take life a bit seriously. Teaching them a certain discipline, a taking of one's self in hand, will provide a foundation that will stand them in good stead all the days of their lives and will lead them to success. However, the discipline should not be taught with too much strictness, for the time of youth is magical, and we should not dim a youth's gaiety, but should seek to make it burn ever more brightly.

60

We are the doorway
through which life unfolds.

wu wei's comment:

Everything we hear, taste, smell, feel, see, or experience in any way is life unfolding through us. To keep aware of that, that it is life we are continually experiencing, will ensure that we are treating each instant with the reverence and wonder it deserves. And in our awareness, if we are joyful doorways through which life unfolds, life will then bring us ever more fulfillment, ever more wonderment, ever more joy.

61

*The way to be happy
is to be happy.*

wu wei's comment:

As free-thinking, free-willed people, we have
the power to choose the way we want to feel. In
every instance, if we choose to be happy, rather
than sad or angry or hurt, we will find that at the
end of a day, a week, a month, a year, a lifetime,
we will have spent a great amount of time being
happy. It takes practice, feeling happy about the
ever enfolding events of life, and, because of all
the conditioning we have undergone before this,
it may be very difficult to make the change, but
if we take the saying to heart and practice it, as
the days unfold we will find ourselves living
ever happier lives, smiling more, and finally,
laughing more.

62

Using our imaginations,
we sow the seeds of our success,
the seeds of our destruction.

wu wei's comment:

We imagine ourselves to be great. Therefore, we think great, act great, and become great. We imagine ourselves as failures. Therefore, we think failure, act failure, and become failures. People who have voluntarily ended their lives did so for only one reason: they used their imaginations to envision a dismal future without end. Other people in the same conditions and circumstances used their imaginations to envision bright, happy, prosperous futures and they survived, they were happy, and they prospered in the bright futures they imagined. It is true that we are in charge of our imaginations, and by using them to imagine wonderful futures for ourselves, and by acting on that basis, it will follow, unerringly, that for us, it will be so.

63

We program ourselves
so that time moves
ever more quickly.

wu wei's comment:

From the time we are young, we are always wishing for time to pass more quickly so we can get to a holiday, the movies, a birthday, a vacation, the end of the school day, the end of pain or an illness, the time for a loved one to arrive, or to an age where some event becomes possible. Being the powerful beings we are, we finally achieve our goal, and time flies ever more quickly the older we become. To slow time down, practice enjoying the moment. It is where we spend our entire lives.

64

*To compose our minds
before speaking
saves us from great error.*

wu wei's comment:

To compose our minds means that we calm our emotions. Speaking in anger, frustration, or without careful thought, often leads to regret and misfortune. We cannot recall the hastily spoken word that destroys the friendship, crushes the heart, or ruins the trust. The thoughtfully spoken word eases pain, brings happiness, stimulates good will, creates courage, renews faith, bolsters a fallen ego, puts laughter in the heart and a sparkle in the eye. Intent is the key word in communication. If we intend that our words do not hurt but bring good cheer, we will speak in a manner that will see us rise high in the hearts of all with whom we communicate.

65

Know the seeds.

wu wei's comment:

The beginning of change is imperceptible. Long before the avalanche cascades down the hill, minute, imperceptible changes have been progressing in the earth. Good fortune and misfortune both have their respective beginnings long before they become evident. It is only after sufficient changes have occurred that we can perceive toward which end our actions will take us. One act does not make a person noble, nor does one act make a person bad. It is only a continued course of action along either of those paths that results in the creation of a good or bad person. Knowing the seeds, the first imperceptible leaning toward good or evil, will find us masters of our fates.

66

Everything that occurs
benefits us.

wu wei's comment:

The continuation of the Universe depends on the law that the best possible event is the only event that can occur. We, being part of the Universe, are benefited by that same law. To keep aware that all events benefit us, and in the maximum amount possible, is one of the most valuable insights obtainable. It is also one of the most difficult of which to keep aware. Knowing that one Universal law saves us from countless hours spent in lamenting seemingly unfortunate events, and lends a rosy hue to all our visions of the future. He who knows that one law and reacts to it accordingly, is nearly a sage.

67

In the times of
greatest prosperity,
decline is immanent.

wu wei's comment:

That is Universal law, which, like all Universal law, is inescapable. Times of prosperity can be lengthened, times of decline can be shortened, but they cannot be avoided. It is also part of Universal law that the greater and longer the time of prosperity, the greater and longer the time of decline. It is only when one has risen to a great height that one can fall from a great height. In times of prosperity, hardly anyone listens to the sage who foretells of the coming change because we are too busy profiting and enjoying the good times. Those who say we have overcome the business cycles are those to whose benefit it is to put out such misinformation. Do not be misled. It is the way of the wise to prepare for the time of decline in the time of prosperity, and he who does so will prosper, and he who does not shall fail.

68

To truly see,
we look with our hearts.

wu wei's comment:

Seeing with our eyes, we see only objects, and not even the objects themselves, but only the light rays reflected from those objects. The light rays, stimulating our optic nerves, forms a picture in our mind's eyes, which we then interpret. It is in the interpretation that the use of our hearts comes into play. It allows us to feel compassion for another's suffering, joy for another's happiness, concern for another's need. It is in seeing ourselves with our hearts that we learn to make allowances for ourselves, to forgive ourselves, to love ourselves as we properly should. For those who see with their hearts, life will truly be an open blossom, filled with delicious nectar and sweet fragrance.

69

To know the future,
see the past.

wu wei's comment:

At the completion of a project, an encounter, a
day, a year, a lifetime, we need only to look
back on our conduct, our intentions during that
time, and the results we achieved to know what
the future holds. If the effects were beneficial, if
the results were good, if our hearts were in the
right place, good fortune is certain. If not,
misfortune follows surely. It is also true that
history repeats itself and cycles are a reality.
Look back to look forward.

139

70

Great and difficult goals
are accomplished
in simple, easy steps.

wu wei's comment:

It is difficult to envision a year. But if we break the year down into months, then days, then hours, we master the visioning. We cannot cultivate a huge field all at once, but doing one furrow at a time will inevitably see the entire field cultivated. To contemplate an entire trek up a great mountain is daunting. However, one step up the mountain is easy to take, and so follow the rest of the steps until the summit is reached. We should therefore not be disheartened by great projects or huge tasks, but we should divide them into small, easily handled tasks and accomplish them one step at a time. We need not concern ourselves about the outcome. All that is necessary is that we begin and continue to the end, one step at a time.

71

The superior person
has purpose
as a way of life

wu wei's comment:

Having purpose means that all our actions are
influenced by an underlying directive force.
Without a directive force to keep us on our
chosen heading, we are blown willy-nilly by
every vagrant wind of fancy. If our purpose is
to achieve enlightenment, our path will be filled
with wonder, and everything we experience will
point to the way. If our purpose is to live the
life of the superior person, all our actions will
reflect superiority, all our results will reflect
superiority, and, as a result of natural law, we
will come to live the life of a superior person,
enjoying its wondrous rewards. We must, each
of us, decide what his purpose will be, and, by
holding fast to it, we will live the life of the
blessed and speed to our goals as hungry
travelers spying the inn.

72

The superior person
looks down upon no one.

wu wei's comment:

Even the weakest or worst among us has been
deemed worthy by the Universe to receive the
rays of the sun, the beams of the moon, and the
bencfits of water, air and the fruits of the earth.
Whom the Universe so honors, should we look
down upon or despise? In the eyes of the
Universe, we are all weak, all frail, all in need of
improvement. Each of us has passed through
many stages, many lifetimes, and where we have
been, and where we are now, others will be or
have been. We are all evolving beings, and to
look with disdain at the place of another is to
become unfit in the eyes of the Universe which
has seen fit to include that person. The most
aware among us progresses along the path with
one hand reaching out in front to receive help
from another and one hand reaching behind to
give help to another.

73

Paying attention
to what is close at hand
brings great progress and good fortune.

wu wei's comment:

We have only so much attention to give. In these days of instant global communication, if we permit it, our attention will be filled with information, most of which is of no value to us at all in our everyday lives, nor does it concern us in any way. If we allow our minds to be filled with such useless information, we will neglect what is near at hand that would be of great use to us. Cultivating one's own garden, paying attention to one's own family, or repairing one's own house is of much greater value than concentrating on the activities of some celebrity, political figure or event that, while it may be interesting, has nothing whatsoever to do with our own lives. Better to mend our socks which has a direct and immediate benefit.

74

The Universe is the great healer

wu wei's comment:

There is a healing force in the Universe which each of us has the ability to use to heal another. To do so, we simply ask the Universe aloud to send its healing energy through us into the person to be healed, then we rub the palms of our hands vigorously together for a few seconds, hold them about a foot above the area to be healed, palms down, and move them slowly about in a circular motion. Our hands will tingle and we will feel heat generated by the friction of rubbing and from the healing energy flowing through them to the other person. After a few minutes of moving our hands in the circular motion, we thank the Universe for the healing and close the session. The healing can be repeated as needed. We should not take credit or payment for such healing as it is a gift from the Universe. That method of healing has been handed down to us from the time of Fu Hsi, perhaps 10,000 years ago, and it is indeed powerful.

149

75

In personal relationships,
affection and consideration
are the main ingredients.

wu wei's comment:

Unlike formal relationships where the duties and rights of the participants are set forth in written documents, relationships of friendship and the heart depend on the consideration and thoughtfulness of the partners, and on their affection for one another. By taking some time each day to bring happiness to those we care about will see our relationships strengthen and grow like strong oaks of the forest.

76

Welcome the dissenters.

wu wei's comment:

It is often the dissenters of life who bring about change. Frequently the dissenters have a valid basis for their dissension that reveals a flaw or injustice in the current system which can then be repaired. Therefore, when we hear a dissenter, we should listen judiciously to his dissent, seeking to see the flaw he sees so that we may address it and improve the situation. For proceeding in that open minded manner, we will be looked upon with great respect, and we will often find solutions that might otherwise escape us.

77

Live in the light.

wu wei's comment:

There is a spiritual space in which we can exist where the light of Universal protection surrounds us.* In that space we are protected from the pitfalls that beset the path of the unenlightened, we succeed rapidly, and even the fiercest attack glances off us harmlessly. Allowing evil or negative thoughts to dwell in our minds or living inferior lives, dims that Universal light of protection, leaving us open to misfortune. Living the life of the superior person causes that light to burn brightly, continuously, and we become invincible.

---

* See wu wei's I Ching Handbook, Chapter 7

78

No need to ask.

wu wei's comment:

To ask for something from the Universe is to
demonstrate awareness and unawareness at the
same time: awareness that the Universe is alive,
aware, and conscious, and unawareness that the
Universe is always completely aware of our
needs and will attend to them at the exact right
moment without our asking. When we have a
need that is a Universal need, meaning one that
is needed for our growth or for our betterment, it
is filled immediately as a function of Universal
law—the best event for our maximum benefit at
all times. If we should ask for something, the
fulfillment of which would deprive us of a
needed opportunity for growth or betterment,
the chances of our requests being fulfilled are
unlikely.

79

Events
are the language of the Universe.

wu wei's comment:

We speak to the Universe with words, thoughts, and actions, and the Universe speaks to us with events. An example of an event is what we call coincidence, although there is actually no such thing in the Universe. A meeting "by chance," is not actually by chance, but by design. Every event is a Universal communication. By acknowledging the Universe each time we become aware of its communication, the Universe becomes aware that we are aware of it, and so raises the level of communication. To be aware that the Universe is constantly communicating with us is to live in a manner only to be thought of as magical, and brings rewards of ever greater significance.

If you would keep your secret
a secret,
tell it to no one.

wu wei's comment:

If we, ourselves, cannot keep our secret, how much less will another?

161

The path of the superior person
is the road
of success.

wu wei's comment:

Some of us talk about the road *to* success, as
though success is a destination. Those who
know, speak about the road *of* success because
the moment we begin the path of the superior
person we are successful, and the Universe,
which is aware of our every word, thought, and
deed, immediately acknowledges our action and
assists us in every way. On the path of the
superior person, we are the embodiment of
success, and all we do begins successfully,
continues successfully, and ends successfully.
How could it be otherwise in a Universe where
cause and effect is the basic principle? We need
take no thought for end results, only that each
step of our way is made by a superior person.
Natural law brings about the only possible
result.

The Poem Of Confucius

Life leads the thoughtful man on a path of many
windings.

Now the course is checked, now it runs straight
again.

Here winged thoughts may pour freely forth in
words,

There the heavy burden of knowledge must be
shut away in silence.

But when two people are at one in their inmost
hearts,

They shatter even the strength of iron or of
bronze,

And when two people understand each other in
their inmost hearts,

Their words are sweet and strong, like the
fragrance of orchids.

(551-479 BC)

The Superior Person

In I Ching Wisdom, Volume I, it is stated:

Every person
must have something to follow,
a lodestar.

wu wei's comment:

Everyone needs something to bring out the best in himself and to provide direction for his development. By holding the image of the superior person in your mind as your lodestar, you will achieve not only supreme success but also great happiness.

A few qualities of the superior person.

He is humble.

He is willing to let others go ahead of him.

He is courteous.

His good manners stem from his humility and concern for others.

He is good-natured.

He is calm.

He is always inwardly acknowledging the wonder he feels for all of creation.

He is willing to give another the credit.

He speaks well of everyone, ill of no one.

He believes in himself and in others.

He does not swear.

He is physically fit.

He does not over-indulge.

He knows what is enough.

He can cheerfully do without.

He is willing to look within himself to find the error.

He is true to what he believes.

He is gentle.

He is able to make decisions and to act on them.

He is reverent.

He carries on his teaching activity.

He does not criticize or find fault.

He is willing to take blame.

He does not have to prove anything.

He is content within himself.

He is dependable.

He is aware of danger.

He is certain of his right to be here.

He is certain of your right to be here.

He is aware that the Universe is unfolding as it should.

He is generally happy.

He laughs easily.

He can cry.

It is all right with him if another wins.

His happiness for another's happiness is sincere.

His sorrow for another's sorrow is sincere.

He has no hidden agendas.

He is thrifty, and therefore is not in want.

He finds a use for everything.

He honors everyone, and is therefore, honored.

He pays attention to detail.

He is conscientious.

He values everyone, and, therefore, everyone values him.

He is optimistic

He is trustworthy.

He is good at salvage.

He is patient.

He knows the value of silence.

He is peaceful.

He is generous.

He is considerate.

He is fair.

He is courageous in the face of fear.

He is clean.

He is tidy.

He does not shirk his duties.

He causes others to feel special.

He expects things to turn out well.

He is always seeking to benefit others in some way.

His presence has a calming effect.

He is not attached to things.

He sees obstruction as opportunity.

He sees opposition as a signpost deflecting him in the right direction.

He sets a good example.

He is joyous of heart.

He takes thought for the future.

He wastes nothing; therefore he always has enough.

He has good manners.

He obtains nothing by force.

He overlooks the mistakes of others.

He has greatness of spirit.

He is clear headed.

He does more than his share.

He meets others more than half way.

He rests when it is time to rest; he acts when it is time to act.

He feels no bitterness.

He is forgiving.

He does not pretend.

He is not cynical.

He studies.

He reveres the ancient masters.

He is inspiring.

He nourishes nature and therefore is nourished
by nature.

He leaves things better than he found them.

He does not make a show.

He practices goodness.

He is simple.

His intentions are always beneficial.

He is a wellspring of determination.

He does not boast.

He produces long lasting effects.

He has endurance.

He is flexible in his thinking.

He does not overreach himself.

He does not overspend himself.

He does not strive foolishly.

He is consistent.

He does not go into debt.

He lives a simple life.

He nurtures his good qualities and virtues.

He is sensitive to his inner prompting.

He exists in the present.

He feels no break with time.

He is cautious.

He is kind.

He holds his goals lightly in his mind, allows no opposing thoughts to enter and, as a result of natural law, is drawn inexorably to his goals.

He seeks enlightenment.

He sets limitations for himself within which he experiences complete freedom.

He is careful of his words, knowing he is reflected in them.

He does not use flattery.

He depends on himself for his happiness.

He feels secure.

He knows the truth of his existence.

He does not strive for wealth, fame, popularity or possessions.

He does not complain.

He turns back immediately having discovered that he has strayed from the path of the superior person.

He practices daily self-renewal of his character.

In I Ching Wisdom, Volume I, it is stated:

Only
through daily self-renewal of character
can you continue
at the height of your powers.

wu wei's comment:

It takes Herculean effort to reach the peak of perfection in any area of life and continuous effort to remain there. Every day some effort should be expended in refreshing ourselves with the ways of the superior person. Reading the I Ching or other great books, talking to like-minded people, teaching others, studying the deeds of our ancient heroes, thinking about our actions of the day to see whether we are being the best we can be, all are ways to successfully continue on the path. As we grow in awareness, our power grows, and our attainments will be like the harvest after a perfect summer. There is no other activity that rewards us as richly as the daily self-renewing of our characters.

Farewell

This is where I leave you, my friend. I am not leaving you in any real sense of the word for, from where we are, there is no place to go. We are here, all of us, eternally. When everyone comes to know that, everyone will act in everyone's best interest. Remember that we are indestructible children of a golden Universe, as much a part of the Universe as the Universe itself.

May you learn quickly, benefit greatly, and attain to sublime wisdom. I wish you love and the greatest of good fortune, and may you mount to the skies of success as though on the wings of six dragons!

Your insignificant and humble servant,